"Let's begin a new chapter in our life journey"

This is a paper book where you can spread out your ideas and more; Enhance your life quality on a daily routine.

By writing on daily basis you can easily improve yourself

Write anything about anything...

WRITE IT DOWN

WRITE IT DOWN

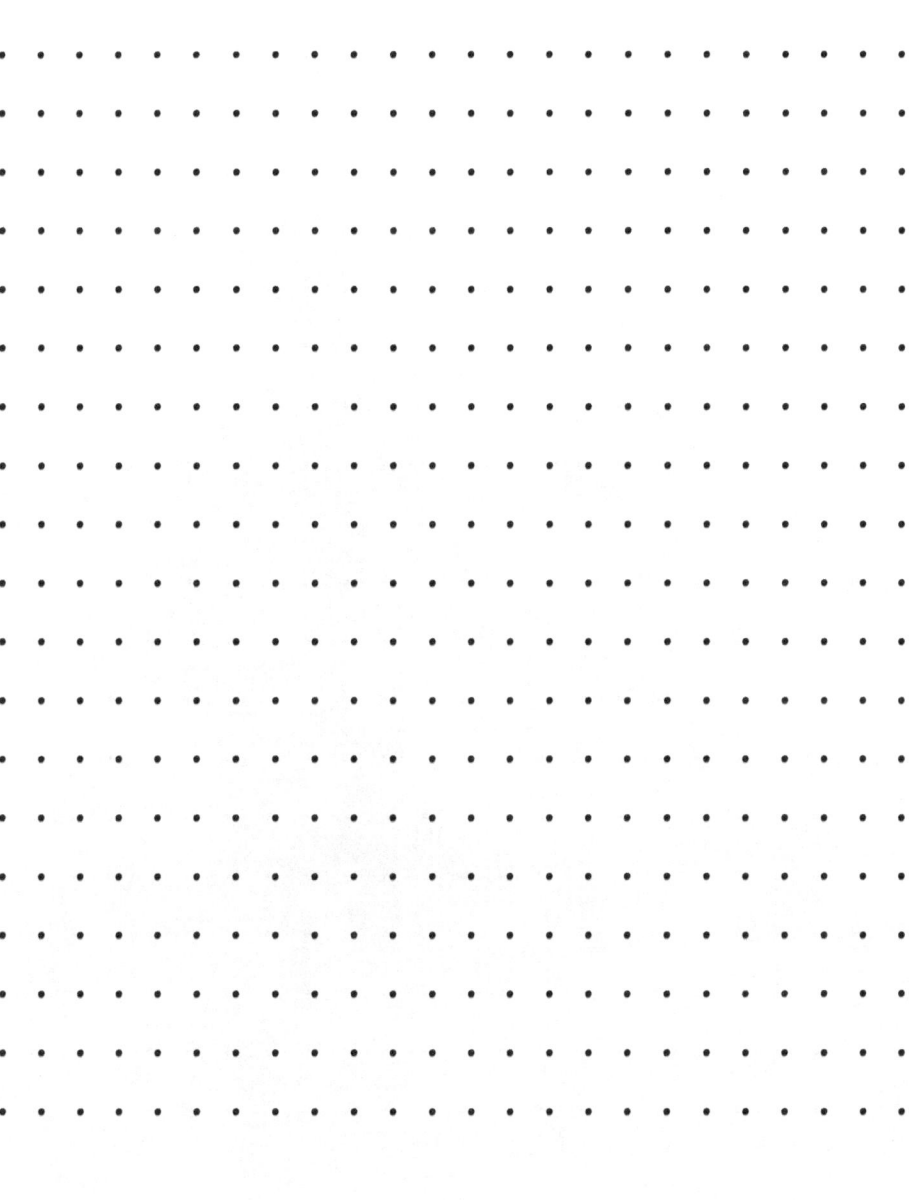

WRITE IT DOWN

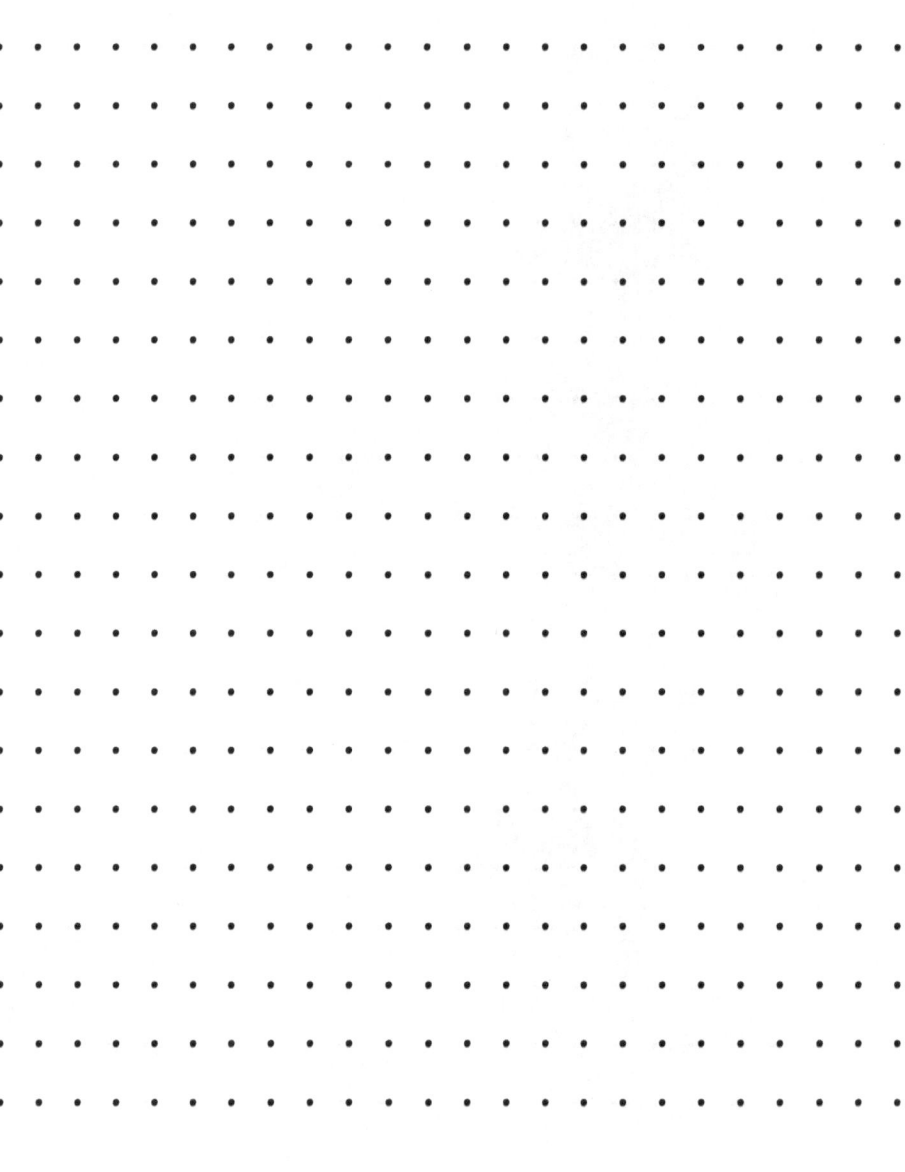

WRITE IT DOWN

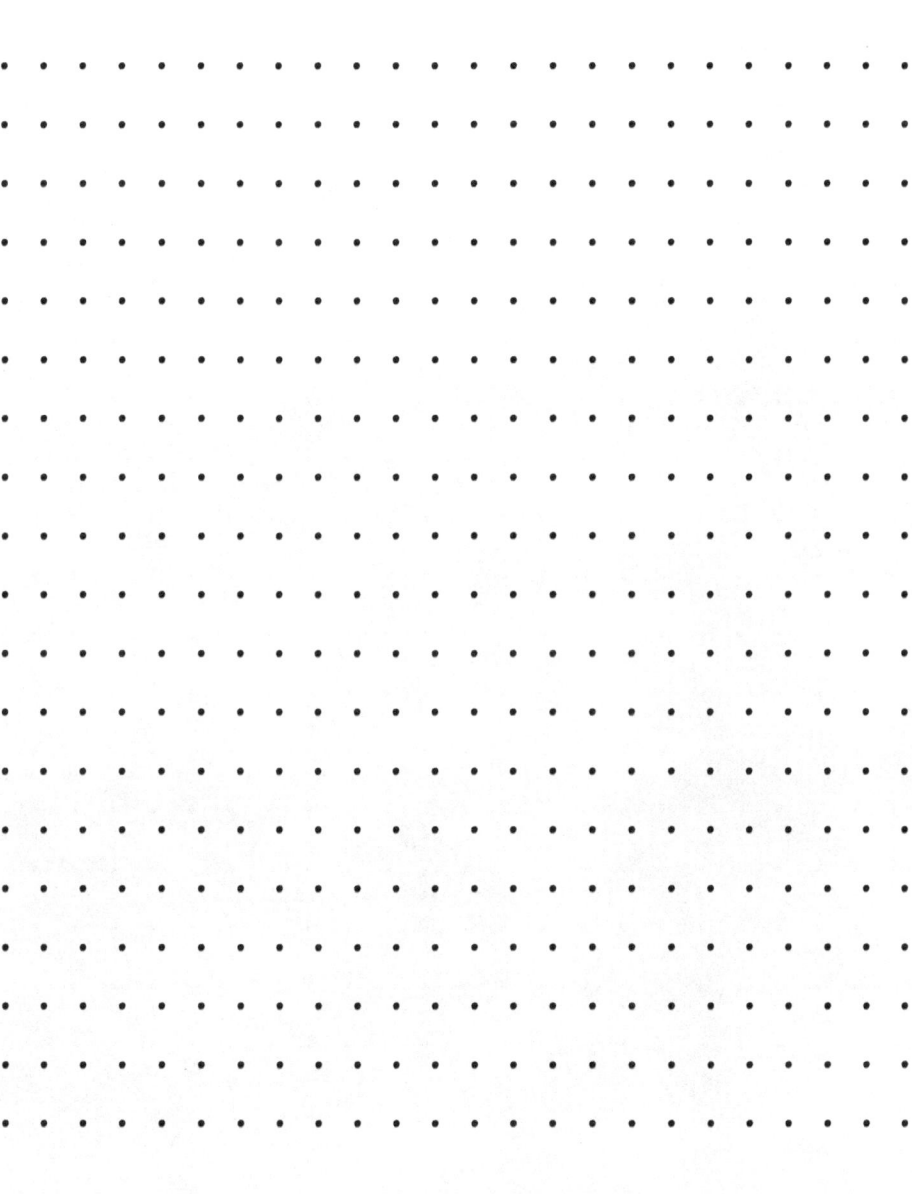

WRITE IT DOWN

WRITE IT DOWN

WRITE IT DOWN

WRITE IT DOWN

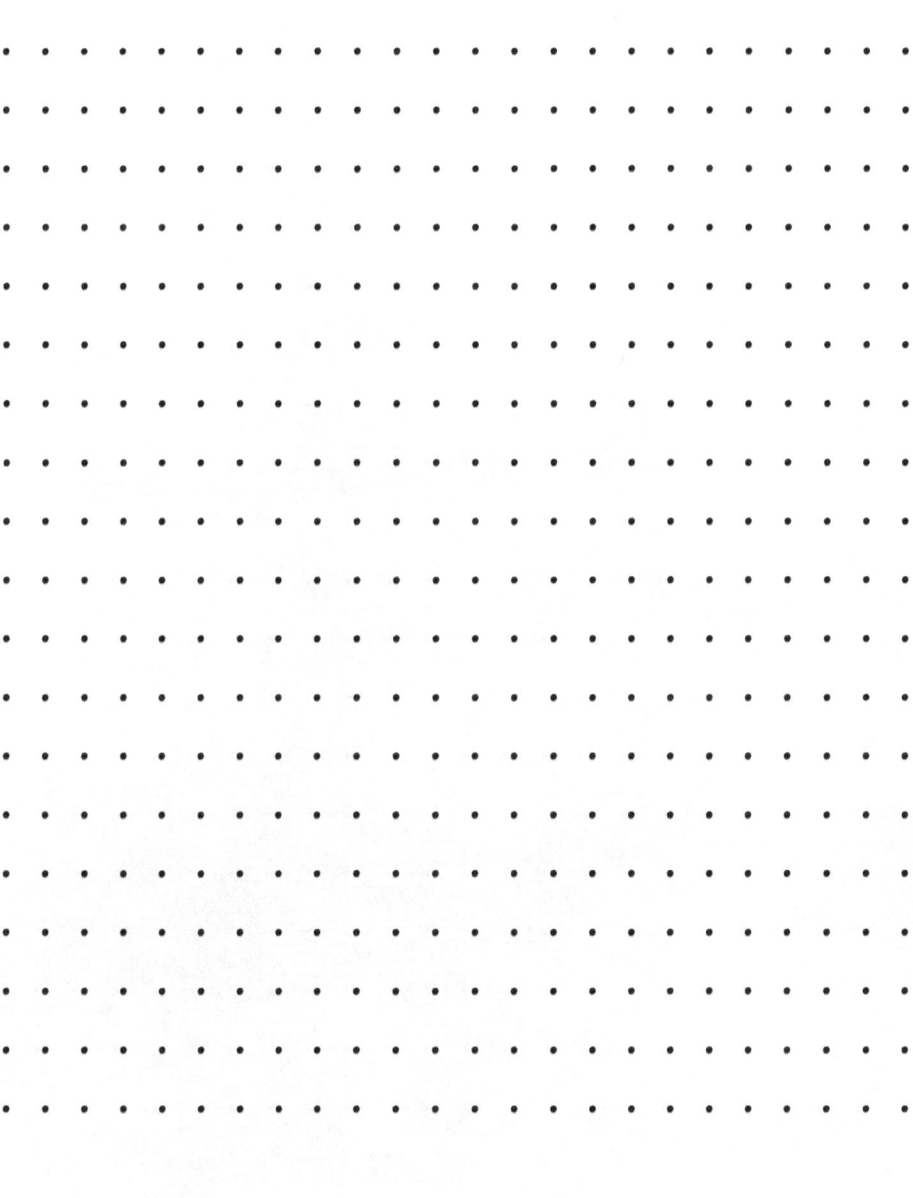

WRITE IT DOWN

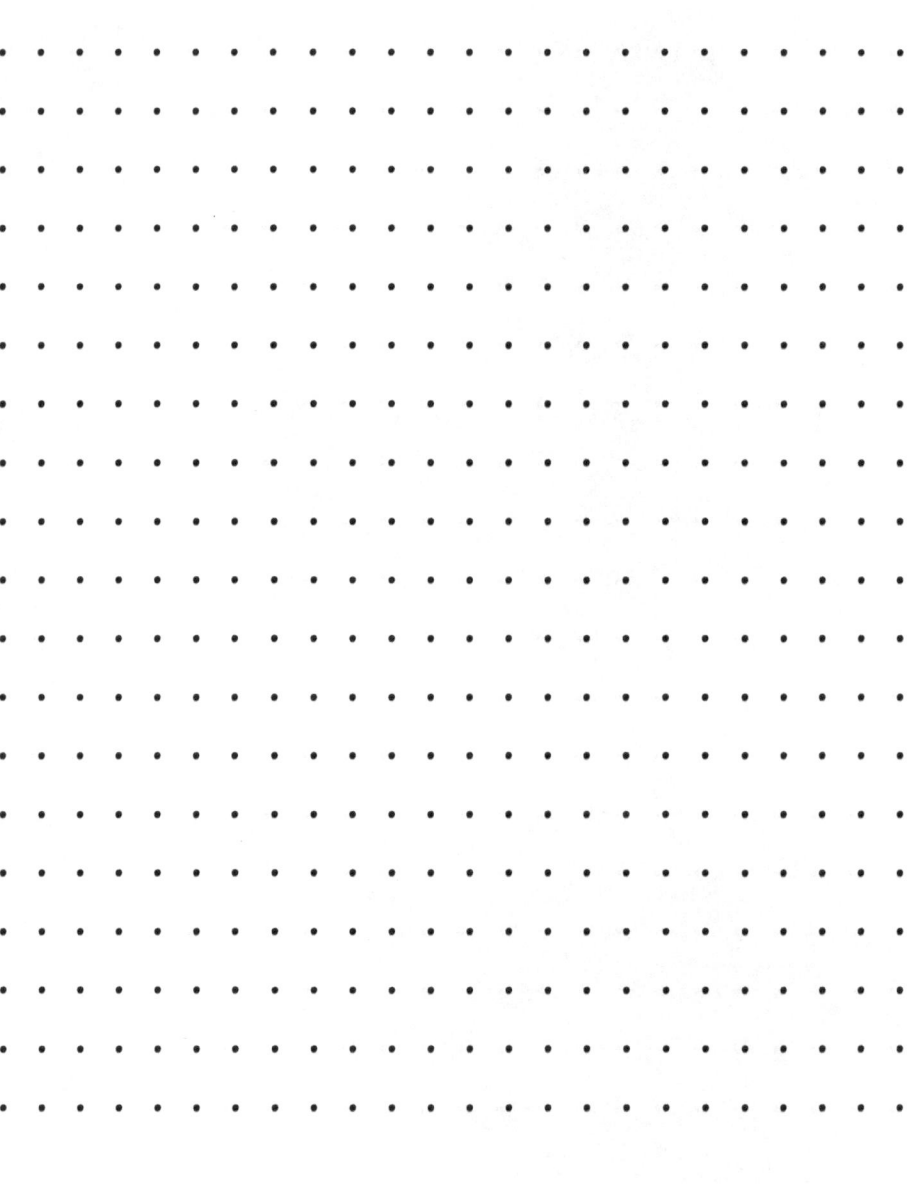

WRITE IT DOWN

WRITE IT DOWN

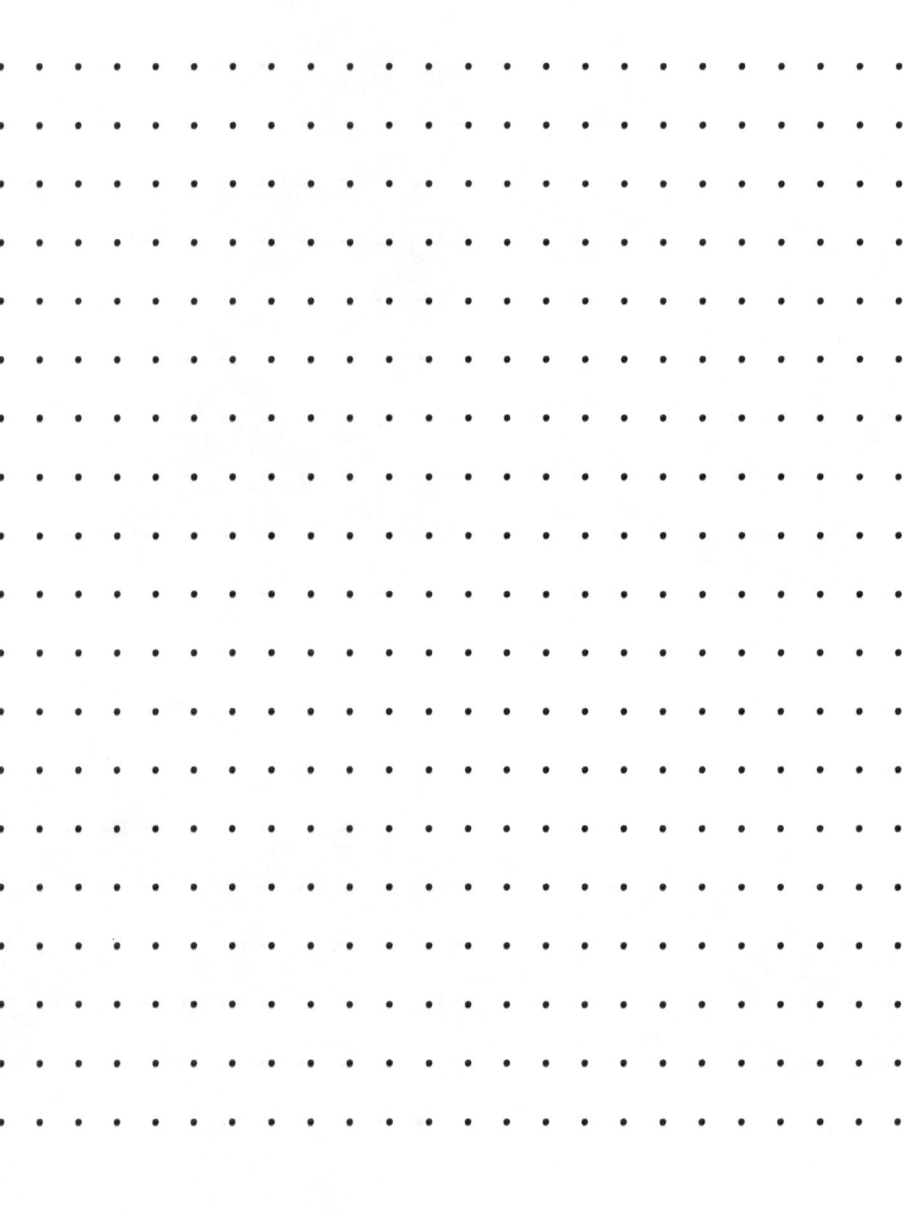

WRITE IT DOWN

WRITE IT DOWN

WRITE IT DOWN

WRITE IT DOWN

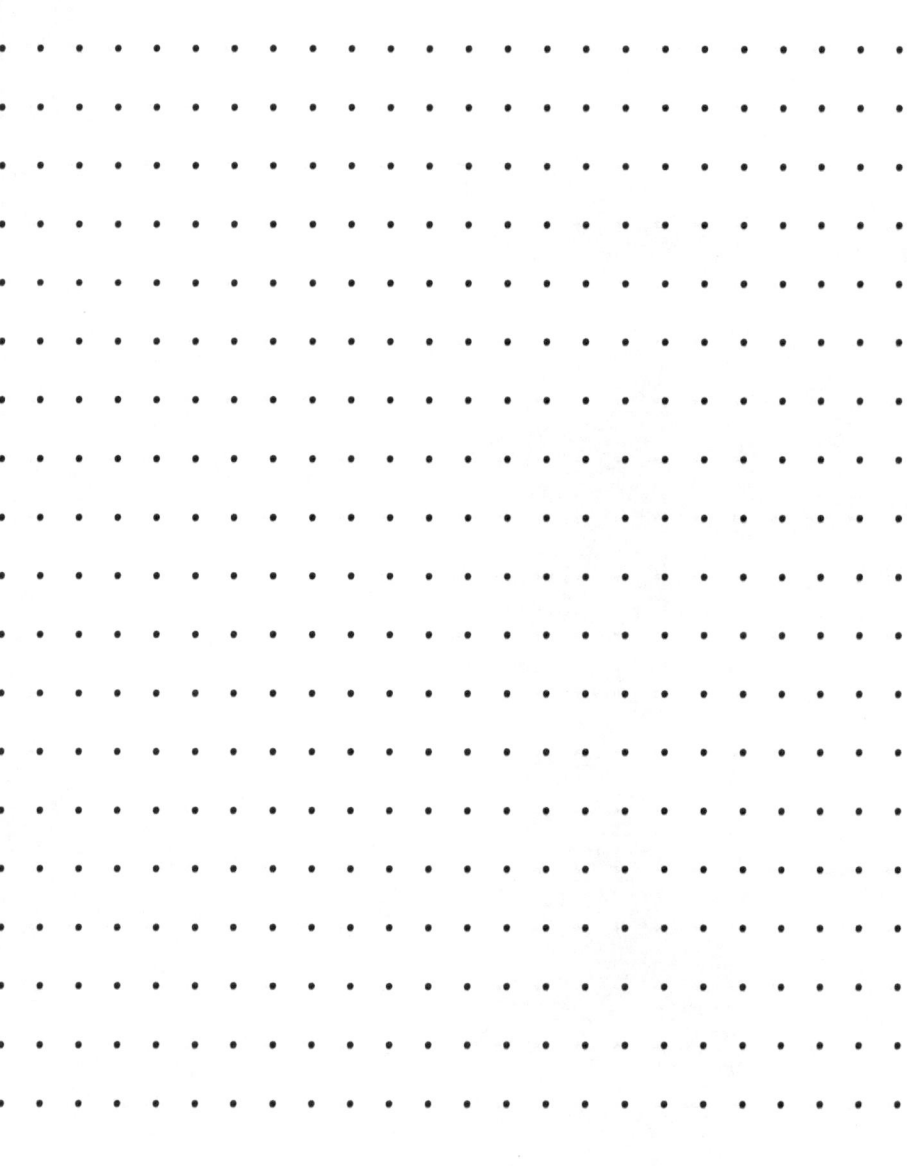

KEEP WRITING

MAKE YOU OWN HABITS

PLAN'S FOR THIS YEAR

10 THING'S YOU LIKE ABOUT YOUSLEF THE MOST

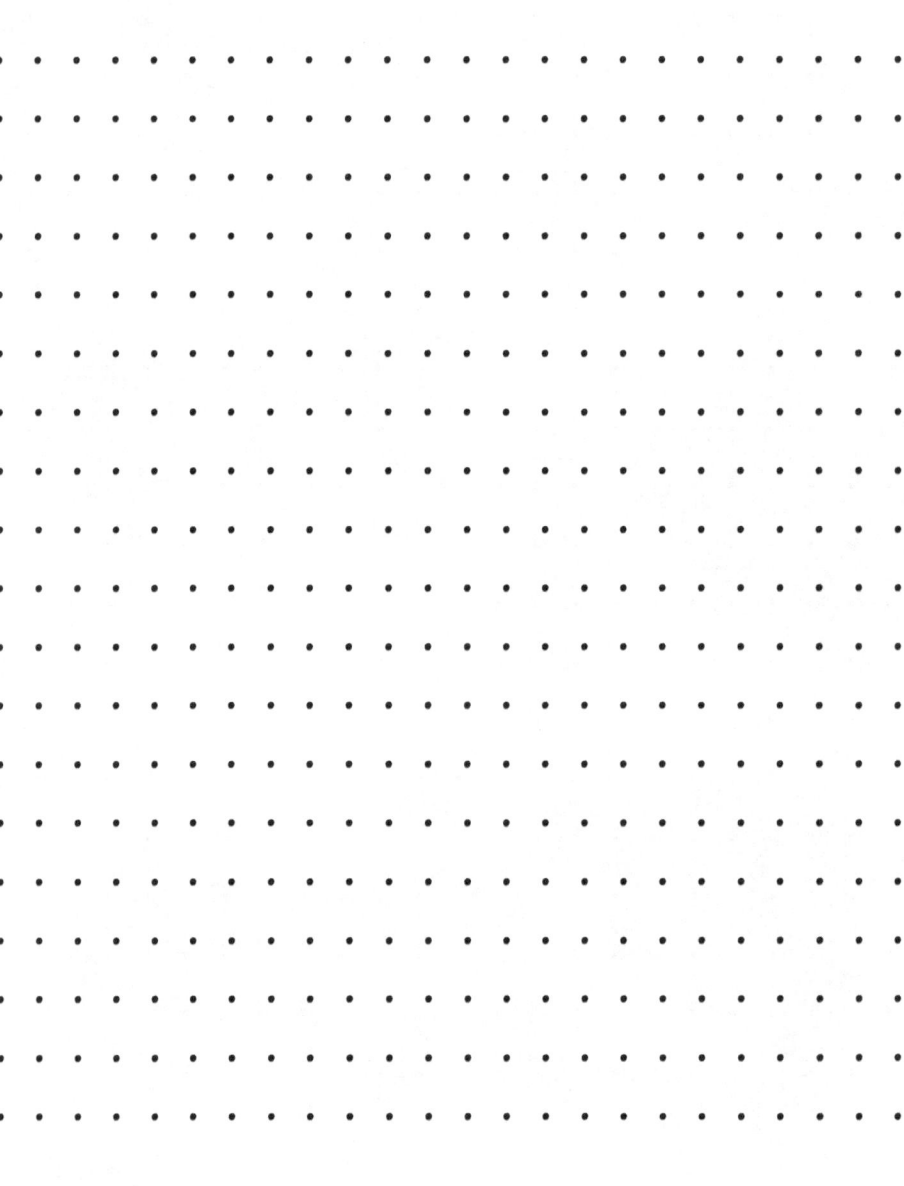

10 THINGS YOU WANT TO IMPROVE IN YOURSELF

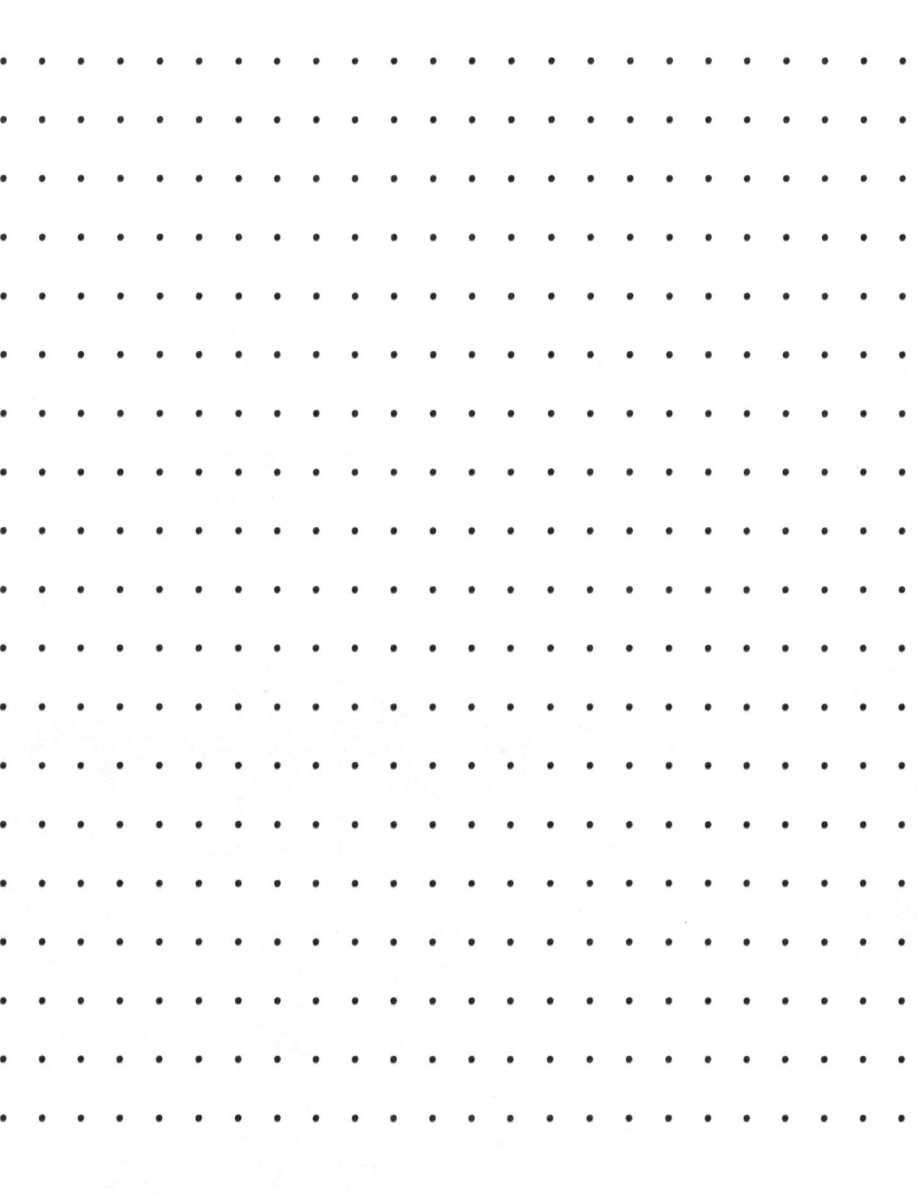

SHARING IS CARING, Till 3 Beloved ONES About This Paper book

. . . .
. . . .

. . . .
. . . .

. . . .
. . . .

YOUR ARE JUST AMAZING
YOU ARE UNIQUE
PUT SOME PHOTOS

YOUR ARE JUST AMAZING
YOU ARE BETTER
YOU ROCK'N'ROLL

www.ingramcontent.com/pod-product-compliance
Lightning Source LLC
Chambersburg PA
CBHW031511210526
45463CB00008B/3186